Planning for Instruction:
A Year-Long Guide

J. Allen Queen
Jenny R. Burrell
Stephanie L. McManus

Merrill,
an imprint of Prentice Hall
Upper Saddle River, New Jersey   Columbus, Ohio

Editor: Debra A. Stollenwerk
Production Editor: Julie Peters
Cover Designer: Diane C. Lorenzo
Production Manager: Pamela Bennett

Printed in the United States of America

10 9 8 7 6 5 4 3 2 1

ISBN: 0-13-021996-7

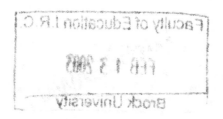

Contents

Acknowledgments

The following students in ADMN 6120 in the spring of 1999 made major contributions to this work.

Chapter 1:	Fred Dobens
	Peter Lambert
Chapter 2:	Miriam Brown
Chapter 3:	Susan Gibbs
	Bob Johnston
	Pokie Noland
Chapter 4:	Ivy Raynard
Chapter 5:	David Fonseca
	Chad Thomas
Chapter 6:	Stephanie Galloway
Chapter 7:	Zhiviaga Saxon
Chapter 8:	Linda Coppedge
	Jeff Hamilton
Chapter 9:	Betty Burrell

Dedication

J. Allen Queen: To all the great teachers who have touched my life

Jenny Burrell: To my parents, Grandmom, and Alice, the best teachers I could have asked for; Julie, for her support, encouragement, and faith in me; Melanie, one of the finest educators I know

Stephanie Liles McManus: To my parents and my husband, who believe knowledge and love are what make life a pleasure. To Sarah Lowder, a true lifelong learner, and one of my "most favorite" teachers

Foreword

Teaching is a wonderful profession in that, each year, you are able to start anew. Whether you are a new teacher or an experienced one, reminders of the basics are helpful to review before beginning each school year, semester, or week. This book contains just the reminders you need as you begin or continue your professional growth in this exciting profession as a classroom teacher.

Remember that teaching is both an art and a science. As an art, teachers use creativity, innovative thinking, and motivation to deliver instruction to students in fun yet exciting ways. But, without science, much of the procedural aspect of teaching is lost. Excellent teachers have both in varying degrees. Strive to be the teacher who discovers the artful aspects of teaching and masters the scientific elements necessary for the successful delivery of instruction to students. By no means is this book a comprehensive instructional or management guide. It simply covers the basic skills needed in the teaching process. In it, you will find tips covering starting the school year, developing long-range and daily plans, classroom management, teaching methods, and time and stress management. It is intended for use as a quick reminder and reinforcement of the "common sense" strategies you need throughout the year.

This book should be used as a starting point—a handbook, if you will. It provides you with a knowledge base that will support your continual professional progress. Periodically, you will come across boxes labeled "For More Information." These boxes can direct you to specific resources that go more in-depth on the subject matter discussed.

Publication of this book has been an interesting process. The topics were selected by working with classroom teachers, supervisors, and principals at all instructional levels. Graduate students with numerous years of experience as classroom teachers provided a good deal of the actual content found in the text. I provided the ideas, the directions, and perhaps the motivation to get the book completed. My co-authors, Jenny and Stephanie, deserve most of the credit for editing the materials from the teachers and graduate students to make a practical handbook for instructors at any level to use. My sincere appreciation goes to all of my graduate students who contributed to this text.

J. Allen Queen

Chapter 1
A Positive Beginning to Your School Year

If a job is worth doing, it is worth doing well.
–Proverb

Perhaps the Boy Scouts of America say it best—"Be prepared." This chapter will share insights as to how you can be ready for the school year. You will learn tried-and-true tips and techniques that will provide the groundwork for a successful year of teaching.

Before the School Year Begins

The first impressions you will make on parents, students, and colleagues are lasting ones. Therefore, taking the time to prepare is of utmost importance. Although your pre-student workdays are busy ones, take the time to talk to experienced colleagues and administrators. From them, you can learn such things as the appropriate attire for your school, where to park your car, and the best and worst routes to take on those traffic-filled mornings. You will save yourself a great deal of time and aggravation.

Following is a list of questions to ask before the school year begins. Keep these notes in a convenient place so that you can refer to them as needed.

* Where do I park?
* Where is the main office? (Note the name of the secretary and get to know him/her well.)
* Where is the counselor's office?
* Where are telephones located (for parent contact)?
* How am I expected to dress? ("Professional attire" can vary subtly among schools.)
* Where is the teachers' lounge?
* Who is my mentor? (Note classroom location and planning time.)
* Who is the chairperson of my department?
* Where are the teachers' restrooms?
* What are typical first-day administrative procedures?
* What is the most efficient route for me to take to school?
* What are some opening student activities that have proven successful?
* Who is the media specialist? (Get to know him/her well.)
* Who is the district's curriculum expert?
* Where do I obtain teacher's editions of textbooks?
* What is the procedure for checking out media equipment?
* What are the fire and other emergency procedures?

Preparing for the Arrival of Your Students

In addition to finding out about your new school, you must also prepare for the arrival of your students. Make sure you take the time to prepare your students' learning environment, your "home away from home." Your classroom should be a welcoming and exciting learning environment for both you and your students.

Student Readiness Checklist

_____ My name and room number are displayed prominently both outside and inside the classroom.

_____ I have a "Welcome" sign of some sort posted.

_____ Classroom expectations and consequences are posted at the front of the room.

_____ I have mini-lessons planned for teaching the expectations and procedures to my students.

_____ The day's assignments are posted on the board (where they will be posted daily for the year).

_____ I have written plans for the first two weeks of school.

_____ I have emergency plans prepared and have notified my principal and a nearby colleague of their location.

_____ I have a temporary roll prepared. (Do not use your "official" roll book for the first few days, as there will be changes.)

_____ My seating chart is completed alphabetically and in pencil (alphabetically to aid in learning names; in pencil to make changes easily).

_____ The bell schedule is posted prominently.

_____ I have drafted a letter to parents of my students explaining my management plan, grading policy, and times I can be reached during the day.

_____ I have information regarding the needs of exceptional children and medical conditions for my students.

_____ I have prominently posted the fire exit route.

The more you can organize before the school year begins, the better. It is a good idea to record important dates for the school year in your planning book. Ask the secretary for a copy of the school's calendar and record the following:

* The beginnings and endings of grading periods
* The days progress and/or report cards are issued to students
* Dates of professional development conferences
* Teacher workdays and vacation days
* Faculty and department meeting times
* Standardized testing dates
* School board meetings

The First Day with Students

Your first day with students is always a hectic one. You will have a great deal of "administrivia" to attend to in addition to introducing your students to your expectations, procedures, and the like. It is a good idea to have one or two activities on hand for the first day to orient students to their new classroom and to each other. Listed here are a few activities you may want to try. Be sure to ask your colleagues about activities they have used.

Activities for Students' First Day

* Scavenger Hunt: Create a scavenger hunt for students to complete on their first day in your classroom. This activity is composed of a list of questions, or clues, that lead students around their learning environment. The questions can encompass posters, expectations, consequences, positive reinforcement, or the location of daily assignments. Students may complete the hunt in pairs or independently.

Sample questions:
What is the third expectation for this class?
Where is the pencil sharpener located?
Where do you turn in makeup work?

* Student Interviews: Give each student a questionnaire to use for interviewing classmates. Questions can relate to favorite music groups or movies, places of birth, and so on. Pair students and give them about five minutes to complete questionnaires. Afterward, students can introduce each other to the class.

* Interest Inventory:	Give each student an inventory to complete. This is a terrific opening activity that allows you to collect information about your students while completing administrative chores such as checking schedules and distributing texts. You can request any information that you may need during the year s uch as addresses, phone numbers, class schedules, and so on. You may also want to ask content-relevant questions.

TIPS FOR SUCCESS

* Greet your students at the door with a smile each day.
* Teach your students responsibility for their actions.
* Model the behaviors you want your students to demonstrate.

Start each day with an assignment that students can begin upon entering class. This provides you time to take roll and complete other administrative duties. Beginning-of-class assignments can be review questions or problems, journal writing, or even copying down the day's assignments. These "start-ups," as some teachers call them, are an excellent way to set the tone for the class.

You should communicate your expectations with parents as early in the year as possible. One efficient way to do this is to send a letter home on the first or second day of school. This letter should include your classroom management plan, grading policies, and times that you can be reached. Most importantly, the letter should let parents know that you plan to work with them in helping their children succeed. For the sake of documentation, it is a good idea to include a signature page for both parents and students. This page, complete with a statement such as "I have read and understand the expectations and policies in Ms./Mr. X's class," can be filed for future use, if necessary.

Never wait to contact parents until there is bad news. Parents are thrilled to be notified of good news!

For More Information

The First Days of School: How to Be an Effective Teacher.
Harry Wong and Rosemary Tripi Wong; Harry Wong Publications; ISBN 0-9629360-0-6.
The 4 x 4 Block Schedule. J. Allen Queen and Kimberly G. Isenhour; Eye on Education, Inc. Publishers; ISBN 1-883001-56-0.

Chapter 2
Time Management

> Spend less time figuring out what's wrong
> and more time doing things right.
> –Bob Algozzine, *Teachers' Little Book of Wisdom*

If you have not already, you will soon discover that there is never enough time to do all the things you need to do. By realizing this, you can learn to use the time you do have wisely. In this chapter, you will learn many helpful time management strategies to help you maintain your sanity in the seemingly never-ending job of teaching.

Planning the Academic Year

In planning the year for your students, you will need to focus your attention on the curriculum guide for your subject. Begin by thinking broadly—that is, in terms of the entire academic year. Some districts have predetermined curricula in the form of pacing guides, which are excellent for developing your long-range plans. However, if you need to create your own guide, you must first study the standards for your school district to determine the curriculum goals for the year. Next, decide how you would like to group these goals. Then, determine the approximate amount of time you need to spend on each unit or goal. (Remember, this is a "guess-timate.") You can then use this pacing guide as a general timeline for your academic year.

A Word of Caution About Long-Range Planning

Count on needing to spend more time on a unit than you think. Build in time "cushions" of a day or two for each unit of study.

Use your long-range "blueprint" to develop your daily and weekly plans in more detail. As you create lessons and units, be sure to keep them organized for use in the future. Many teachers find that maintaining a three-ring binder for each unit is a good way to keep lessons and units orderly. In addition, you can jot notes in these unit notebooks about what worked, what did not, and what you would like to try. If the idea of preparing notebooks sounds too involved, try maintaining file folders—they take even less time to organize!

Remember that it is worth the extra time to put materials for a lesson together; the next time you use that lesson, you will know where to go and what to try.

Using Spare Time to Your Advantage

To preserve your sanity throughout the year, you will need to use each precious minute that becomes available to you. Believe it or not, there will be times when you find yourself with a *few* spare minutes! Taking advantage of these small amounts of time will help you feel more in control, less overwhelmed. To best use the spare moments, you will need to have work readily available. Keep folders in a designated area, such as your desk drawer. Label them according to task. You may have one for materials that need to be copied, one with student papers to be graded, and one general "To Do" folder. When you find some time, grab one of the folders and complete as much as you can. Make sure you keep stick-on notes handy to mark your place when you are interrupted. Keeping work organized makes it easy to access during those spare moments.

Another great way to spend small amounts of time is to jot down class plans. If, as suggested in the first chapter, you write your daily class plan in the same place each day, you'll have your list ready to transfer to the board. Just this simple listing can save you time when you are preparing for the next day. The busy life of a teacher makes it easy to forget things. Jot them down whenever you get the chance and put your notes in a designated place to minimize the threat of teaching-related "amnesia."

A Sample Class Plan Listed During Spare Time

For Tomorrow:

1. *Start-up activity: Capitalization Rule #5*
2. *Take up language homework (p. 41)*
3. *Review vocabulary words for "The Monkey's Paw"*
4. *Discuss foreshadowing / take notes*
5. *Read "The Monkey's Paw"*
6. *Work in analysis teams to complete plot & characterization activity*

You may wonder where you will find time during your busy day. Perhaps homeroom has been extended, your students are reading silently, or their art lesson is running late. Learn to be on the lookout for bits of time that you can use. One caution about these small amounts of time—never count on them! Instead, welcome this extra time as a nice surprise and take full advantage of it.

Focus

- **Utilize all available time!**
- **Keep work accessible!**

Using Time Outside of Class

Those beautifully executed lessons you teach in your classroom are often developed outside of class (indeed, often on your "own" time). Teaching can be a twenty-four hour a day job. No matter how much you have done, you can always find more to do—more research, more planning, more conferencing, more responding to students' work. Where do you set boundaries? When have you done enough? What is the total time each week you should budget for your duties? This is difficult to determine and requires good judgment on your part.

Many teachers find that their workweek is much more than the typical forty hours. Take into consideration the time you spend working after school and at home. You probably work a few hours each day in addition to class time. If you find yourself spending so much time that you feel you do not have your own life, you need to figure out what is eating up your time and how you can remedy it. Your administrator, mentor, or another close colleague may have some insight into how much time you should spend outside the "normal" school day. Remember, even as a devoted teacher, you need and deserve time for family, friends, relaxation, and personal growth. See Chapter 8 for more in-depth coverage on this subject.

Making Parent Contacts More Efficient

Parent contact will be never-ending. Remember that all contact does not necessarily need to be made by phone. You may decide to send a letter home or schedule a face-to-face conference, depending on the nature of your contact. In the letter you send home at the beginning of the year, you may want to provide a place for parents to write down when, where, and how they would prefer to be contacted. No matter what form of contact you choose, you must take time to document it. If your school does not have a form for keeping track of parent contacts, you should make a simple contact log which includes the student's name, the date and time of contact, the form of contact, and the outcome of the contact. This log will prove valuable when meeting with parents or administrators about particular students. Another use for the log is to show you how much of your time is spent on parent contact so that you can better budget your time.

Helpful Hints on Parent Contact
- Do not call only when there is a problem; parents love and need to hear good news, too!
- Consider sending positive notes home in the form of postcards; some schools send "Cool Grams."
- Try your best to make contact with each and every parent/guardian throughout the year.

In this day and age, you have a variety of communication methods to choose from when contacting parents. However, no matter what form your parent communication takes, document it. If you send a letter, make sure you photocopy it and place it in the student's folder. Follow up if you do not believe the letter was received. Some parents may prefer to be contacted via e-mail. Make certain that you print copies of all messages to and from parents for your records. To save time on phone calls, which can be the most time-consuming method of communicating with parents, prepare a brief statement of the student's progress and conduct before placing the call. Be prepared to give parents a specific time for them to contact you if more information or follow-up is necessary. Consider setting a boundary on phone contacts by limiting them to two evenings per week.

A Word of Caution About E-mail Contact

Be careful not to dash off angry messages. Write out your message first, then reread it and send it a while later. E-mail contact lacks facial expression and voice tone; it can be easily misunderstood.

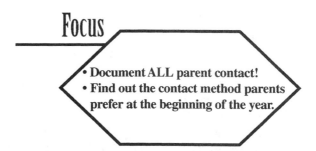

Focus

- **Document ALL parent contact!**
- **Find out the contact method parents prefer at the beginning of the year.**

Grading Student Work

Perhaps the most time-consuming of all teacher work is grading. Since grading gives you, your students, and their parents feedback, the best use of grading time should maximize the information gleaned. In addition to using the aforementioned strategies, you can save time by using selective grading and rubrics. In selective grading, you may choose only certain items or aspects of assignments to grade. In addition, you may opt to have students complete a few activities and then announce which one will be handed in and graded. Select the items/assignments from which you can obtain the most complete assessment of your objective. Remember that, although it may go against your instincts, sometimes you need only check for simple completion. In addition, you may occasionally discover that a particular assignment is not even necessary.

Following is a list of additional time-saving grading ideas.

Ways to Save Time on Grading

1) Student Self-Checking

Students highlight what they miss, and you can glance to see what further instruction is needed. This is great for practice exercises.

2) Checking Station

You provide an answer key and turn-in basket, and students write the number incorrect at the top of the page. You can have students show you their completed work beforehand if you are concerned about cheating.

3) Computer Quizzes

If you are lucky enough to have a computer lab, check out what software programs are available. Some provide quizzes for various subjects. The results can be printed out and handed in to you. Ask your technology specialist about what is available to you.

4) Spot Grading

Announce to students what the focus of your grading will be. This way, you will not need to check every detail of every paper. You can determine the most important features relevant to your lesson. For example, if your language arts class has been studying topic sentences, you may decide to focus on that area for a particular writing assignment.

For More Information

Life Strategies: Doing What Works, Doing What Matters.
Phillip C. McGraw, Ph.D.; Hyperion Publishers;
ISBN 0-7868-6548-2.
Slow Down...and Get More Done. Marshall J. Cook;
Betterway Books; ISBN 1-55870-270-9.
Seven Habits of Highly Effective People. Steven Covey;
Simon and Schuster, Inc.; ISBN 0-671-66398-4.

Chapter 3

Designing Instruction

> Education is what survives when
> what has been learned has been forgotten.
> –B. F. Skinner

Remember the instructional design course from your undergraduate study? The knowledge gained there will become valuable as you spend a good portion of your time planning instructional units for your students. In the broadest sense, instructional designs are a compilation of learning activities that are intended to ensure student learning, accomplishing the goals and objectives of the curriculum. These units will obviously vary as the depth of study varies and as your goals and objectives vary for your students. Remember that plans that are a "perfect fit" for your students this year will need adjustments for next year's student population.

As you plan, take into account the varied learners for whom you are planning. Use your knowledge of learning styles as you plan for the different individuals in your classroom. Also, integrate learning from other disciplines so that students understand how learning relates throughout various curricular areas. In some way, relate the learning to the individual's life and interests so that each student sees a connection between the learning in the classroom and life goals.

The Importance of Designing Instruction

Remember the Boy Scout motto "Be prepared"? Here that old adage rings true again. Designing instructional units helps you be ready for school on a daily basis and beyond. You design the instruction based on the information you have regarding curricular goals and demands of future goals and experiences that await your students. Always keep in mind that your curricular area does not exist in a vacuum. You are helping to prepare students for a future that is definitely integrated. However, this does not mean that you should omit a particular unit if you cannot find ways to integrate it with other subjects. This means that if there is a connection, do not avoid it. If a connection would prove helpful to your students in a planned study, by all means, integrate.

Using the Designed Units

Planning will be your lifeline to solid instruction. The design of a unit will enable you to focus on what your students need to learn to succeed in a particular study. Your designed units will enable you to plan various activities to ensure meeting the needs of various types of learners. It will also ensure that all of the goals and objectives that you intend to cover are included.

Although you may alter your plan somewhat, you must first get it down on paper. Wouldn't you rather have a written plan that you have to change a bit to make fit the needs of students than have a plan somewhere in your overworked, overstressed brain that you just cannot access at the moment?

Focus
- Plan it!
- Write it!
- Do it!

"Where Do I Start?"

A common concern of novice teachers is the beginning—the beginning of school, the beginning of a wonderful lifelong career, and the beginning of an instructional unit. Everyone wants each beginning to run smoothly. How do you start to plan an instructional unit? The best way to begin is to carefully study the curricular materials produced and/or provided by your state, your district, and your school. These documents tell a great deal about the goals and the standards by which your students—and you—will be evaluated. Most states offer standard course of study books that detail goals and objectives for the various grade levels and subjects. Some states that mandate statewide testing also publish support materials that provide helpful instructional pointers as well as models for you as you plan your instruction. All of these documents should be available at your school site or through your district office. Above all, do not be afraid to ask for help; this is as important for you to remember as it is for your students.

Instructional Unit Components

Generally, instructional units are designed around basic components. It is necessary to keep these in mind as you plan, design, and integrate the instructional program. Following is a list of the general components of designed instructional plans.

1) Theme—the focus of the major content to be taught
2) Main Expectation—cumulative outcome desired for the students
3) Rationale—the reason or need to teach the particular topic
4) Task Analysis—division of larger topic into smaller teachable tasks
5) Main Objectives—come from the task analysis and are a sum of the main expectations throughout the lesson
6) Coding Procedures—used in integrated units to tie certain

lessons and activities to various subject objectives (for example, one activity that ties in objectives from social studies and language arts); objectives can be coded with the abbreviation of the subject and the number of the objective

7) Lesson—should be designed to take time necessary to implement enabling activities; will last one to several days, depending on the objectives and intended outcomes

8) Closure—should be a true wrap-up and culmination of the knowledge and skills imparted

9) Student Assessment—the process of formal and informal measurement of the success of the achievement

Analyzing Goals

Once you have finished establishing your goals through the help of various support documents and support personnel, it is time to begin the planning of tasks to reach your particular goals. What types of experiences will your students need to reach the set goals? What smaller set of objectives will be needed to reach the standard of learning you have established? See the following example for clarification.

Example

Your topic is penguins, and you want your students to write a descriptive paragraph of at least six sentences. You may analyze your tasks as follows.

Task 1—Students will be able to write complete sentences with correct usage of capitalization and punctuation.

Task 2—Students will demonstrate knowledge of where penguins live, what they eat, what they look like, and how they reproduce, by explaining these in writing.

When you analyze your goals for your students and determine the tasks involved in reaching the goals, you will have created your list of objectives—the building blocks of solid instruction.

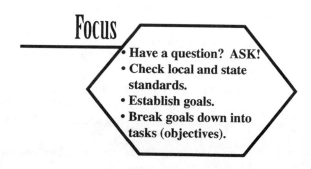

Focus
- **Have a question? ASK!**
- **Check local and state standards.**
- **Establish goals.**
- **Break goals down into tasks (objectives).**

Determining the Effectiveness of a Lesson

How will you know that students have achieved the goals you have set for them? How will you know that you have helped students meet or exceed standard? How will you know they are able to "pass the test"? You will evaluate them, of course!

Although assessment typically comes at the end of a unit of instruction, you should think about assessment during your planning stage. Do not make it an afterthought. How can you plan instruction without knowing at the same time what the ultimate goal of that instruction will be? So many varied tools exist to help assess students' growth. Use those and create your own.

Assessments vary in scope, depth, and time constraints. Choose one that best fits your need and the standard you have set for your students. Assessments range from informal to formal. You will use informal assessment (such as oral questioning) every day. Take care not to make it the only type you use.

Methods of Assessment

Oral Questions	Observations
Informal Dialogues	Traditional Quizzes
Tests	Open-ended Prompts
Application Scenarios	Extended Prompts
Performance Tasks	Projects/Presentations

Assessment is covered more in-depth in Chapter 6. It is mentioned here so that you are clearly aware that assessing is part of planning good instruction. It is not a separate entity.

For More Information

Creative Teachers, Creative Students. John Baer; Allyn & Bacon; ISBN 0-205-19568-7.
Designing Effective Instruction, 2nd edition. Jerrold E. Kemp et al.; Prentice-Hall, Inc.; ISBN 0-13-262080-4.
Principles of Instructional Design, 4th edition. Robert M. Gagné et al.; Harcourt Brace Jovanovich College Publishers; ISBN 0-03-034757-2.

Chapter 4

Developing a Daily Lesson Plan

Genius is one percent inspiration and ninety-nine percent perspiration.
–Thomas Alva Edison

Think of instructional design as two parts. The first part is the unit design—the big picture. The second is the daily plan—the smaller, more detailed picture. The units are like a large road map that gets you from state to state. The lesson plans are city maps that navigate you through the details of your journey. Without the details of your journey—daily plans that accomplish objectives—you would not reach the destination—your larger instructional goals.

Daily lesson plans are key to good instruction and successful teaching. These plans affect the very nature of the activities within the classroom. Taking time, therefore, to plan thoughtful lessons is essential. This chapter includes information on

- Components of daily lesson plans
- Formats for planning
- Considerations when planning
- Resources for daily planning

Confidence and Communication

Logical, easy-to-follow plans prevent you from experiencing unstructured class sessions and classroom chaos. Good planning does take time. However, good planning results in clear, concise lessons for which teachers project confidence. That confidence aids classroom instruction and classroom management. When the focus of the classroom is on student outcomes through well-planned lessons and activities, more time is spent on task, and—teachers will testify—student achievement rates are generally higher.

A Note About Classroom Chaos
Many behavior problems stem from instructional flaws, which are caused by poor planning.

Planning daily lessons gives you an organizational tool as well as a communication device. You are able to quickly review your lessons as the time nears to prepare particular materials. You are also able to demonstrate the growth and depth of studies over the course of the year.

Although perfectly organized plans do not guarantee good teaching, they certainly enhance the chances by detailing what is to be taught. This organizational format also allows for professional dialogue about goals, materials, outcomes, and successful methods.

Remember that the purpose of your planning is to help students learn. Be willing to monitor and adjust if your plans are not working. Monitoring, evaluating, and adjusting your instruction are necessary in a "true" teaching/learning environment. Do not be so determined to teach a well-planned lesson that you spent hours on that you are willing to sacrifice student learning. The goal in planning these daily lessons is student accomplishment.

Some good reasons for preparing thoughtful daily plans . . .

More time spent on task by students
Greater command of subject content by teacher
Organizational tool for teacher
Communication tool for teachers, colleagues, administrators

Components and Formats for Planning

You may use a specific lesson plan format designed by your school district or department, or you may create one of your own. Some schools and school systems mandate a certain type of form. Be aware of those mandates and comply with them. If you need help in converting a planning format you are comfortable with to one that is mandated for you, let someone in your department or an administrator know.

Although there is great variety in lesson plan formats, all planning should include the basic components of prerequisite knowledge, instructional objectives, instructional delivery and practice, procedures, materials and equipment, student assessment, and self-assessment. Keep in mind that the format is not as important as what the lesson contains and accomplishes. Understand that a lesson may take two, three, or even more days to complete. It is important to give your students enough time to truly learn the material and skills.

A sample daily planning format follows.

Daily Lesson Plan Format

Teacher_____Class_____Date_____Topic_____

Prerequisite Knowledge/Skills

Instructional Procedures
       1) Lesson Introduction (review/statement of objective)

       2) Delivery (teacher input—instruction and then guided
                practice)

       3) Student Independent Practice and Assessment

       4) Closure

       5) Reinforcement/Enrichment (individualization)

Materials (teacher and student)

Teacher Self-Assessment

Note. This plan format has been condensed to fit into the limited space.

As you continue to plan, the task will become easier. You will grow more comfortable with the process and will likely develop your own format and style. However, make sure you always include the aforementioned components, whatever the format.

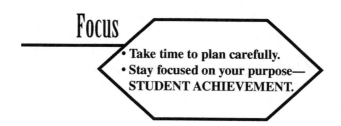

Focus
- Take time to plan carefully.
- Stay focused on your purpose—
  STUDENT ACHIEVEMENT.

A Special Focus on Block Scheduling

Schools are increasingly adopting block scheduling. This form of scheduling can impart a dynamic framework to create a safe school and a productive learning environment. With block scheduling, there are fewer class changes and a reduction in discipline referrals, thus improving the school environment. The student/teacher ratio is decreased as well, so teachers can focus more on the individual needs of their students.

Strengths of Block Scheduling

• More time for projects, research, and videos
• Students prepare for fewer subjects at a time
• Better use of facilities
• Better variety of electives
• Exploration of more subject areas
• Longer engaged instructional time

Block scheduling does require a change in planning, which is why it is mentioned here. Typically, teachers are with their classes for ninety minutes at a time. Following is a planning guide to assist your pacing during a ninety-minute class.

Pacing Guide for a Ninety-Minute Period

Teacher: _____   Subject: _____

School: _____   Period: _____   Semester/Year:_____

Objectives, Skills, and Competencies	Instructional Strategies and Student Activities	Procedures
	1-10 mins.:	Statement of Objective
	10-30 mins.:	Presentation/Delivery
	30-50 mins.:	Small Group Discussion/ Planning
	50-80 mins.:	Student Presentations
	80-90 mins.:	Summary/Closure

Student Assessment

Planning Considerations

As you plan a lesson, some key factors need to be studied. The following information about your students should always be considered:

> Ages
> Population (demographics)
> Socialization skills
> Grade levels
> Achievement levels
> Learning styles

Of these, two of the most important factors are learning styles and levels of achievement.

Learning Styles

Strive to use a variety of methods in each and every lesson so that you address the learning styles of each student. Three main learning styles are as follows:

1) Visual: Sight is very important to these individuals. They need to see to understand.
2) Kinesthetic: These individuals must be able to put their hands on something, to feel an object in order to learn; some even need to physically move their bodies to learn well.
3) Auditory: These individuals can listen to something and recall, understand, and use the learning.

Achievement Levels

It is important to be knowledgeable about each student's achievement level. One word of caution here: Do not believe that just because a child is labeled "gifted" that she will have no problem learning or that she will be well-motivated. Accurately diagnosed learning problems should serve as guides, but should not be excuses or stigma. With that said, this information is usually located in the child's cumulative folder. If you feel that this type of information will taint your opinions, it may be wise to delay your right as an educator to "dig" through files until you have a true need to know more about a child.

Domains of Learning

It is also important to consider a learner's domain of learning. What you must do while planning instruction is consider that you will have students at various levels within each domain at one time. Of course, that type of a classroom is not a perfect world, but it certainly is interesting. Three domains to focus on are the cognitive, affective, and psychomotor.

Cognitive Domain

This domain is tapped when your objectives focus on students reproducing, remembering, and applying information that was previously learned. For this domain, it is important to consider Bloom's taxonomy. Benjamin Bloom believes that learning capabilities are hierarchical in nature, ranging from the lowest level of cognitive thinking to the highest level of processing and evaluating. When planning, keep in mind the goals you set for your students. The lowest level is knowledge level— "simple" memory. The highest level of cognitive processing is evaluation. While not all students will reach the evaluation level, your goal should be to move beyond the comprehension level of processing. What follows is a chart listing levels of learning, as well as verbs that will make planning objectives easier.

Bloom's Taxonomy Applied*

Level of Taxonomy	What the Learner Does at This Level	Verbs for Planning
Knowledge	Remember previously learned material	Define, identify, label, list, match, select, state
Comprehension	Understand content material	Distinguish, explain, infer, summarize, paraphrase
Application	Apply learned material in real world situations	Demonstrate, modify, solve, use, manipulate
Analysis	Take apart complex ideas and understand relationships	Relate, differenti- ate, separate, break- down
Synthesis	Put items together to make a completely new whole	Combine, compose, create, design, generate, organize
Evaluation	Judge the value of materials	Appraise, conclude, criticize, justify, interpret

*Adapted from Harry and Rosemary Wong's *The First Days of School* (see p. 10).

Affective Domain

A student's affective domain deals with personalities and attitudes. Within this domain, a teacher can create opportunities for lifelong changes for students as the students form opinions that govern action throughout life. If you are not familiar with the affective domain, search out information about this area. The more you know about learning domains, the more benefits your students will realize.

Psychomotor Domain

The psychomotor domain of your learners encompasses their proficiency in motor skill development as it pairs with mental action. Skill at keyboarding is just one psychomotor area. Within the skill development, students must first **familiarize** themselves with a skill, and then follow the next steps:
- **Fundamental** - Basic skills are accomplished.
- **Development** - Practice for control and style occur.
- **Adjusting and adapting** - Skill is "individualized" for proficiency.
- **Perfection and maintenance** - Practice continues for improvement and mastery.

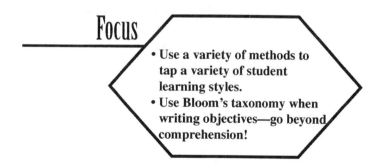

Focus

- **Use a variety of methods to tap a variety of student learning styles.**
- **Use Bloom's taxonomy when writing objectives—go beyond comprehension!**

So many resources exist for you as you prepare your various lessons. Use a variety of sources as you plan. Develop creative lessons from which all students are able to gain. It is imperative to use your sources wisely. Why reinvent the wheel? Teachers should and do share their ideas. Do not be afraid to take someone's idea and use it. Adapt it if you have to and make it your own so that your teaching is the best possible for you and your students. Following is a list resources for you to access. As we have mentioned, every source is just that—a source, a beginning. Make it fit the needs of you and your students.

    1) Colleagues - Do not be afraid to ask for help. Be sure to share the ideas you have, as well.

    2) Mentors - Establish a relationship with someone you feel may help you become the teacher you want to be. Ask that person if you can come to him/her for guidance periodically. Then share the good, the bad, and the ugly. Chances are this mentor has had the same, or a similar, experience. You may be assigned a mentor. If that is not the person you have chosen, think of your situation as lucky! You have TWO people to help you!

3) Professional Journals - These journals offer much advice about methodologies as well as sample lessons. Many articles are written by classroom teachers. For a start, see the listing of journals in this section of the text.

4) Internet - This is a powerful instrument in today's society. You will see the benefits and the disadvantages of this tool as you continue your teaching. Plenty of helpful websites exist. Some even have ready-to-use lesson plans. A word of warning here: Websites are easily made and are not regulated as are other publication arenas. Beware! Some who publish websites are knowledgeable and responsible; others are not. Make sure you thoroughly study the material from a website before you use it with students. In addition, you will also experience the temporary nature of Internet sources as you continue using this tool. There is a list at the end of this chapter of the more reliable sites that may prove helpful in lesson preparation. This list is only a representation of the vast number of sites available.

Professional Journals/Periodicals

- *Art Education*
- *American Secondary Teacher*
- *The American Biology Teacher*
- *Classroom Computer Learning*
- *Classroom Computer News*
- *The Clearing House*
- *The Education Digest*
- *Educational Leadership*
- *Educational Research Quarterly*
- *Educational Technology*
- *English Journal*
- *Gifted Child Quarterly*
- *Harvard Educational Review*
- *The History Teacher*
- *Journal of Education*
- *Learning*
- *Phi Delta Kappan*
- *Teaching Exceptional Children*

Internet Websites

Great Zoo Information
  http://www.geocities.com/~brohm/
  http://sesmoney.ed.asu.edu/~hixson/index/zoo.html
White House
  http://www.whitehouse.gov/WH/Welcome.html
Special Education Plans
  http://www.kodak.com/global/en/consumer/education/lessonPlans/
        indices/specialEducation.shtml
Lesson Plans—various topics
  www.thegateway.org
  www.nationalgeographic.com
  www.askeric.org
Behavior Management
  http:/keirsey.com/abuselose.html
Kindergarten—Great integrated units and lessons
  http://www.kconnect.com/
Language Arts
  http://www.proteacher.com/070000.shtml
Elementary Units
  http://www.proteacher.com/020010.shtml
On-line Lesson Plans
  http://teachingonline.org/unitslibrary.html
Lesson Plans by Subjects
  http://www.indiana.edu

Chapter 5
Dynamic Instructional Strategies

The important thing is not so much that every child should be taught, as that
every child should be given the wish to learn.
—John Lubbock

You will teach many students throughout your career, each and every one an
individual; therefore, you can safely assume that each learns in a different
way. You want to reach all of your students. Increase your odds by learning
a variety of instructional strategies for use in your classroom. The more
strategies you employ, the better your chances of reaching all of your
students and expanding their knowledge. However, you must not toss
strategies into your curriculum without studying them first. This chapter
gives an overview of several methods of teaching. At the end of this
section, you will find a list of sources that cover these methods thoroughly.
Learning and, most importantly, mastering a variety of instructional
strategies are imperative to your growth as a professional. Keep in mind that
you cannot master strategies in only a few uses, and practice makes perfect... or much *better*, anyway!

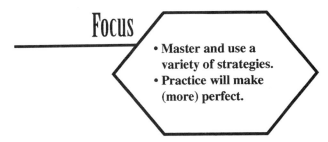

Focus

- **Master and use a variety of strategies.**
- **Practice will make (more) perfect.**

Strategy One: Role Playing

You are probably already familiar with the concept of role play. It involves
learners acting out a situation with the result being resolution of a problem
and/or further comprehension of subject matter. Translated into a classroom
setting, it can be a powerful tool for teaching students problem solving skills
and allowing them to explore individual perceptions, attitudes, and values.

```
┌─────────────────────────────────────────────────┐
│        Basic Guidelines for Role Playing        │
│                                                 │
│   1. Explain the concept to students.           │
│   2. Introduce the situation.                   │
│   3. Assign clear roles and observer tasks.     │
│   4. Discuss the outcomes of the role play.     │
│   5. Discuss issues that should become prominent│
│         through the role play activity.         │
└─────────────────────────────────────────────────┘
```

Strategy Two: Cooperative Learning

Cooperative learning is another strategy that you are probably quite familiar with. When done correctly, this strategy creates small learning communities that prepare students for their future jobs and relationships. Books and theories abound on cooperative learning methods. Ideas vary widely on topics from how large the group should be to the amount of teacher intervention needed. In general, you are wise to begin cooperative learning with your students in small (two to three student) groups.

Arm yourself with a strong knowledge base in cooperative learning. This strategy is not as simple as grouping students randomly or according to their personalities. It involves teaching social skills and using methods to foster interdependence as well as other social structures.

```
┌─────────────────────────────────────────────────┐
│   Basic Guidelines for Cooperative Learning     │
│                                                 │
│   1. Make sure that each student understands    │
│      his role.                                  │
│   2. Clearly define tasks so that students      │
│      remain focused.                            │
│   3. Closely monitor each and every group's     │
│      progress.                                  │
└─────────────────────────────────────────────────┘
```

Strategy Three: Mnemonics

Your students will need to memorize a good deal of information, no matter what your subject. You do not want them to memorize information only for a test or quiz. They need to internalize and assimilate this knowledge. (Remember Bloom's taxonomy.) To facilitate assimilation, a variety of cues and sensory experiences must be tapped. Memory assists are simple teaching tools that work in complex ways.

There are several memory assist systems you can use to help your students memorize and retain subject matter, and they all work primarily by associating unfamiliar material with familiar. Some methods are link-word, ridiculous association, substitute-word, and key word. As you can guess, the names of these are indicative of the methods themselves. It would be impossible to go into detail as to how each works, so following are general characteristics of effective memory assists.

```
┌─────────────────────────────────────────────┐
│             Memory Assist "Musts"             │
│                                               │
│   1.  Draw the learners' attention and focus. │
│   2.  Use cues to develop connections.        │
│   3.  Practice recall and expand sensory      │
│       experiences to enhance retention.       │
└─────────────────────────────────────────────┘
```

Strategy Four: Simulations

Of course you know what a simulation is! Why should you incorporate it into your lessons? Students often want to know "why"—why they must learn algebra, why they must learn to spell when computers do it for them, and so on. Practice of a real-life event brings a resounding answer to your students' questions of "why." Simulations make clear to students the transfer to real life. Your students will learn from the consequences of their actions, or lack thereof.

Simulations can take the form of games (remember the game of *Life*?). In addition, they can be cooperative or individual activities. Simulations, often used in the medical and flight fields, also provide students opportunities to learn from mistakes without actually causing catastrophes.

```
┌─────────────────────────────────────────────┐
│          Basic Simulation Procedures          │
│                                               │
│   1.  Present the concepts of this technique. │
│   2.  Present the situation.                  │
│   3.  Assign roles and practice.              │
│   4.  Conduct activity.                       │
│   5.  Discuss and summarize.                  │
└─────────────────────────────────────────────┘
```

Strategy Five: Advanced Organizers

The name "advanced organizer" is self-descriptive. Introduced at the beginning of a lesson, advanced organizers provide a foundation for higher-level concepts that will be presented later in a different manner. This strategy brings connection and continuity to your lessons.

Providing students with a basic introduction to a lesson is not an advanced organizer. The advanced organizer is typically more abstract in nature than the learning material itself. This strategy takes a good bit of preparation.

```
┌──────────────────────────────────────────────────┐
│      Basic Procedure for Advanced Organizers      │
│                                                    │
│   1. Prior to the actual lesson, present the       │
│        organizer by identifying it and giving      │
│        examples.                                   │
│   2. Present the lesson.                           │
│   3. Have students summarize, define terminology,  │
│        answer questions, give additional examples, │
│        and relate the organizer to the material    │
│        learned.                                    │
└──────────────────────────────────────────────────┘
```

Thinking Maps is a conceptual teaching method that partners a specific organizer with a specific higher-level thinking skill. These are ways for students to connect a level of thinking which can be abstract with a more concrete, visual map of the thought(s).

Strategy Six: Inquiry

You have likely had experience with this method of teaching, as it has come to the forefront in recent years. The premise is to engage students in an investigation of some sort which leads to data gathering. When used correctly, this method incites a desire within students to solve the problem, whether or not it is actually solvable.

It is important to note that activities are not inquiry when *you* are the one who identifies the problem and formulates the investigative strategy. In addition, the *process* of inquiry is of primary importance, not the outcome of the investigation.

Strategy Seven: Group Investigation

The strategy of group investigation combines both the cooperative learning and inquiry approaches. In using this strategy, your students will investigate subject-matter problems while becoming aware of others' points of view. The problem can be presented orally or experientially. Students will be exposed to a variety of interpretations and combine these to broaden the inquiry.

Strategy Eight: Synectics

Even if you do not recognize the name of this strategy, you are probably at least a little familiar with it. Synectics encourages higher-level thinking through the use of analogies. As the instructor, you present the structure for the analogy, and your students participate in open-ended discussion and creative problem solving. For example, a technology teacher may ask students to compare the human brain to a computer.

For More Information

Models of Teaching, 5th edition. Bruce Joyce and
Marsha Weil; Allyn & Bacon;
ISBN 0-205-19391-9.
***Teaching Methods for Today's Schools: Collabora-
tion and Inclusion***. J. Scott Hewit and
Kathleen S. Whittier; Allyn & Bacon;
ISBN 0-205-15413-1.
***Strategies for Teachers: Teaching Content and
Thinking Skills***, 3rd edition. Paul D. Eggen
and Donald P. Kauchak; Allyn & Bacon;
ISBN 0-205-15011-X.
Learning and Teaching: Research-Based Methods,
3rd edition. Paul D. Eggen and Donald P.
Kauchak; Allyn & Bacon;
ISBN 0-205-27089-1.
Learning Theories for Teachers, 5th edition. Morris L.
Bigge and S. Samuel Shermis; HarperCollins
Publishers; ISBN 0-06-040674-7.

Chapter 6
Assessing Student Learning

The test and use of man's education is that he finds pleasure
in the exercise of his mind.
–Jacques Barzun

Improving education is a goal throughout America today. We as educators are expected to produce students who are capable of facing and meeting the standards of an increasingly demanding workplace. In an attempt to measure growth and learning, many states across the country have implemented standardized testing for grade levels and courses. At the national level, groups of standards have been formed that indicate on average where, for example, all fifth grade students should be in their achievement and skills base.

These are all circumstances that you will face as you begin each year with your students. It is important to stay abreast of current trends in standards development. However, what is more important to you on a day-to-day basis is the set of assessment tools you choose to use with your students. Be careful not to simply test memory. Bloom's taxonomy can guide you as you begin to formulate a "testing" situation for your students. Use the ideas you find in the taxonomy to decide for yourself what type of assessment you should implement to measure the growth of your students for a particular concept. Pay particular attention to the sample verbs in the Bloom chart.

SOMETHING TO THINK ABOUT....
- How appropriate is the assessment strategy
  you use for each goal?
- Are you really testing what you teach?
- Are you really discovering true growth for
  your students in a relevant area?

As you plan assessments to coordinate with your goals and objectives, keep in mind that there are as many assessment types as there are students. Not every student will do well on every type of assessment. For this reason, it is important to vary your testing instruments. Tests can be formulated to meet all learning styles. Remember, you are testing the students' achievement as well as your teaching. From one assessment, you may realize that one area you taught did not "catch" as it should. It is then that you must reteach.

This chapter lists only a few of the more well-known categories and types of assessments. The information here is only a beginning. Search out more information as you need it to perfect your assessing capabilities.

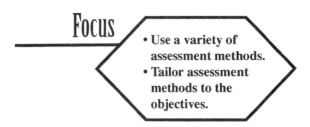

Focus

- Use a variety of assessment methods.
- Tailor assessment methods to the objectives.

1) Standardized Tests - These are the types of tests most likely provided with your textbook. They test various levels of processing. States and institutions use a few standardized tests to compare student ability and achievement. Examples of standardized assessment tools include the following:

- SAT I and SAT II
- ACT
- California Achievement Test
- Comprehensive Test of Basic Skills
- Stanford Achievement Test

You must become familiar with the school, district, and state standardized tests that affect you. The information you gain prior to teaching should prove beneficial as you plan to better serve the test preparation needs of your students.

2) Cooperative Learning Assessments - These activities provide students a challenging task of working together to meet an objective. Be careful how you use this assessment. Remember that your goal here is to stress the importance of collaborating and communicating. These areas should be stressed before the outcome is assessed. Some group assessment types are

- Team projects
- Small-group inquiry discussions and reports
- Debate teams

3) Authentic Assessments - These assessments are sometimes deemed "nontraditional." However, when carefully planned to fit with the goals and objectives, they can be the most appropriate for you as a classroom teacher. The test that actually proves that a student could really change the oil in a car is the one that has him do just that. Such is the premise behind authentic assessment. Teach what needs to be learned, and then test accordingly.

Some sample authentic assessments are	
• Lab reports	• Video tapes
• Created stories	• Songs
• Portfolios	• Sketch
• Business letter	• Tying a shoelace

During your time as an educator, you will meet students with various needs. Some needs are greater than others. Special classroom modifications may be necessary to improve and enhance the academic and learning experiences of certain children. If this is the situation, modifications should be carefully chosen to meet the needs of your students as you give them the most authentic experience possible.

In summary, always remember to accurately assess what you teach by tailoring your assessments to the objectives.

Chapter 7

Mastering Classroom Management and Minimizing Inappropriate Behavior

The best defense is a good offense.
–Benjamin Franklin

Perhaps the biggest worry among teachers is classroom management, and for good reason. There is one of you, the teacher, and twenty or more students. Take the time to develop a comprehensive classroom management plan, and you will be able to breathe much easier the rest of the year. Although you cannot be prepared for every little thing that happens in your classroom, you can be prepared for a great deal.

Your management plan should have four components: procedures, expectations (rules), consequences, and positive reinforcement. In this chapter, you will learn about each of these areas and begin mastering management skills.

Procedures: Building Your Offense

One way to drastically reduce the odds for inappropriate behavior is by developing procedures for your day-to-day class activities. Consistent use of procedures ensures that your classroom runs smoothly and you can concentrate on the real reason you are there—teaching your students!

Procedures differ from rules in that they are the way certain activities are done. Rules have consequences, while procedures are taught until, ideally, they become habit for your students. If a student does not follow a procedure, then you should remind her immediately of the correct method and have her follow it correctly.

Classrooms are busy places. Before beginning the school year, consider all the different tasks that will take place in your classroom on a daily basis. Students will sharpen pencils, need to use the restroom, enter late, leave early, listen to school announcements, complete and turn in work individually and with partners and groups, be dismissed, transition between activities, and so on. Sounds like this could be chaos, doesn't it? It does not have to be. Take the time to plan procedures for common daily activities and teach them to your students. This will prevent a good deal of frustration throughout your year.

Of course, depending on your grade level, your procedures will differ. The beauty is that, with procedures in place and well-taught, instruction is not unnecessarily interrupted.

Create Procedures for Your Classroom in Three Easy Steps

1. Make a list of daily activities for your students. Some ideas are listed below, but keep in mind that your list will differ according to your teaching style and school policies.

- √ Restroom use
- √ Beginning the class period
- √ Getting the class's attention
- √ Getting missed work after absence
- √ Leaving the classroom
- √ Turning in work
- √ Listening to schoolwide announcements
- √ Classroom discussion
- √ Sharpening pencils
- √ Transitioning between activities

2. Prioritize your list according to degree of use. Those procedures used most often will need to be taught first.

3. Decide on a procedure for each activity. As you do this, think, "How can my students go about this activity without the teaching/learning process being interrupted?" See the examples below.

Activity: Sharpening Pencils
Student Procedure:
1. Raise pencil and point to sharpener.
2. Wait for signal (nod) from teacher before sharpening.

Activity: Restroom Use
Student Procedure:
1. Students are given two restroom passes at the beginning of each grading period. (Passes have teacher, room number, place for teacher signature, student signature, and date; they can be color-coded by class and/or semester to prevent inappropriate use.)
2. To use them, students take one out, sign and date it, raise it, and wait for teacher to come sign at an appropriate time.

Your procedures will not work if they are not taught. Take time at the beginning of the school year and after brief holidays to not just tell students what the procedures are, but to teach them. Each procedure should be explained, modeled, taught, and practiced. Students will need to be reminded at first.

Elements to Include in Procedure Mini-Lessons

1. Explain the need for the particular procedure.
2. Model the procedure.
3. Have a student or two perform the procedure.
4. Review.

Do not overwhelm your students by teaching them all of your procedures at once. Procedures are best taught as they are needed. On the first day or two of school, teach a couple of the most commonly used procedures, such as sharpening pencils and beginning the class period. As situations warrant them, teach the others. Remember, however, that students will not automatically catch on to procedures after only one lesson. Take time on following days to review.

Tips for Success

The first week or two of school, remind students of procedures just before they will be used. For instance, a few minutes before the dismissal bell, tell students, "Don't forget the end-of-class procedure!"

Classroom Expectations: AKA "Rules"

Many teachers have found that keeping the number of expectations to a minimum is helpful. Your students are more likely to retain a short list, perhaps of three to five. Since this list is brief, the content is vital. You must decide upon three to five rules that cover what you consider the most important areas of behavior.

A good way to determine your classroom expectations is to ask yourself what your students absolutely have to do/not do in order for you to effectively teach them. If your list is too long, attempt to combine rules. If combining rules is not possible, read over your list and see if one or more rules are actually procedures. Revise your list of expectations accordingly.

As with your procedures, make sure you explain the reasons for each rule you have. The rules are for the benefit of students; they are not a way to get students in trouble, as some students may think.

You may even consider allowing your students to participate in the development of rules on the first day or two of school. Explain the reasons they are necessary and have them discuss what would be appropriate. Some teachers find that this method gives students a sense of ownership that contributes to the desired classroom atmosphere.

A Note About Classroom Rules

Check the faculty and student handbooks before determing your classroom expectations. Get approval from your principal as well. Some schools have predetermined class rules and/or consequences that should be followed.

Focus

- **Keep list of rules short!**
- **Consult administrators before implementation.**

Consequences: AKA "Crime and Punishment"

It is absolutely imperative that you be consistent with respect to consequences. Your students are likely to see your inconsistencies as favoritism. Your classroom consequences should be consistent with those of your school.

Doling out consequences is not a pleasant task. However, it is necessary if you are to maintain an active learning environment. Your students are individuals, and consequences that work with some students may not work with others; therefore, you may find yourself providing varying consequences throughout the school year. You will need a list of consequences from which to select. (Again, your school may have standard consequences you must use—check with your mentor or principal.)

Sample Consequences

- ♦ Detention time before or after school
- ♦ Detention time at recess or lunch
- ♦ Isolation within the classroom

Positive Reinforcement: Rewards vs. Bribes

The positive reinforcement component of your management plan is to reinforce students for good behavior and achievement. It is necessary for you to consider the difference between rewarding your students and bribing them. Students are not necessarily made aware of specific rewards until they actually attain them. Rewards are a pleasant surprise for a job well done, while bribes are dangled in front of students from the beginning—"Please, Jon, if you will just be quiet for ten minutes so I can teach, I'll give you a homework pass!" Bribes may work at times, but they provide only extrinsic motivation. You want your students to be intrinsically motivated, to love learning and to experience the pride of accomplishment. Even though you may choose to provide your students with external rewards for learning, guide them toward intrinsic motivation.

Sample Rewards

◆ Praise

◆ Postcards or letters home

◆ Certificates

◆ Stickers

◆ "Student of the Week"

◆ Cool pencils, pens, erasers

◆ Calendars

◆ Listening to music

◆ Five free minutes

◆ Media center pass

Note: As always, have your principal approve your entire management plan before giving rewards.

For More Information

*Responsible Classroom Management for Teachers
    and Students*. J. Allen Queen et al.;
    Prentice Hall; ISBN 0-13-442336-4.
Punished by Rewards. Alfie Kohn; Houghton
    Mifflin Co.; ISBN 0-395-65028-3.
Classroom Management for Secondary Teachers,
    4th edition Edmund T. Emmer et al.;
    Allyn & Bacon; ISBN 0-205-20005-2.
*Classroom Management for Elementary
    Teachers*, 4th edition Carolyn Evertson et.al.;
    Allyn & Bacon; ISBN 0-205-20006-0.
Classroom Management: Theory and Practice,
    2nd edition Robert T. Tauber; Harcourt
    Brace College Publishers;
    ISBN 0-15-501317-3.

Chapter 8
Building Strong Professional Relationships and Avoiding Teacher Burnout

I touch the future. I teach.
–Christa McAuliffe

The relationships you develop with your colleagues can prove lasting, rewarding, and stress-reducing! Although you teach behind a closed door, you are, together, in the business of educating the nation's youth. This can be a stressful and frustrating job at times, but with trusted and dedicated professionals to turn to, those frustrations can be drastically reduced. However, you will most likely see teachers leave due to "burnout" caused by the stress and frustration. This chapter provides you with some basic methods to assist you.

Building Strong Professional Relationships
Despite how you may feel at times, you are a professional. You care deeply for your students and want to do your best for them as their educator. Experienced colleagues can provide wealth of advice. Indeed, your colleagues provide the foundation for your professional development. Unfortunately, you will find that some teachers are full of negativity. Steer clear of them! Things are not as bad as these nay-sayers would have them seem. Focus on the positive, truly professional colleagues, and you will maintain your own positive attitude.

Your school's support staff is vital; do not neglect to build good relationships with them. Secretaries, custodians, and paraprofessionals play an integral part in the daily operation of the school. Your relationships with them will prove beneficial to your mission of forging strong relationships. Recognize the support staff by showing them your appreciation for all they do.

Cultivate your relationships with administrators through communication. The administration should be informed proactively; use memoranda and e-mails to notify them of your progress, procedures, and problems. Make sure the administration hears of any conflicts from you first, rather than from a parent or even another teacher.

At the district office level, you should certainly get to know the curriculum coordinators. Share your classroom successes with them. Contact them by phone, memo, e-mail, or appointment.

Avoiding Teacher Burnout

One of the most exciting days of your life was your first day teaching. After years of preparation, your goal was achieved. You eagerly planned lessons, created bulletin boards, and prepared for the year ahead. You knew that the educational system needed you and you would make a difference. You had faith in yourself and in your students and were looking forward to building successful relationships.

The first month of school probably brought you alternate highs and lows. Some days you may have wondered what you were doing wrong or even why you had chosen teaching as a profession. Other days seemed to fly by, and you felt disappointment and surprise that the day had ended! You must cope with your lows and learn from them. As stated earlier, go to a trusted colleague; he or she may have just the advice or empathy you are needing!

Recognizing burnout is not easy. Every job has its good days and bad, so how can you tell if what you are experiencing is, in fact, burnout? Trust close family, friends, and colleagues if they express concern about you, as you do not always recognize that something may be wrong.

Burnout or Just a Series of Bad Days?

Answer the following questions. If you answer "yes" to several, you are likely entering the "Burnout Zone."

Do you judge yourself too harshly?
Do you expect yourself to be perfect?
Do you feel you should be doing more, even though you are working hard?
Do you worry excessively about school, your students, their problems?
Do you find yourself bored, even though there is work to be done?
Do you refuse to try new methods and strategies?
Do you find yourself disliking staff and/or students?
Do you withdraw from colleagues and/or students?
Do you feel you made a mistake in choosing to become a teacher?
Do you find yourself constantly ill?
Do you wake up in the morning dreading going to school?

If you think you may be headed for burnout, try some of the following strategies to remedy the situation:

• Focus on your successes. It is entirely too easy to spend a great deal of time focusing on problems. See the glass as half full!

- Plan and prepare thoroughly. This can give you confidence and will help ensure that your classes run smoothly.

- Communicate and collaborate with colleagues. They can offer reassurance as well as advice.

- Allow yourself to be less than perfect. Teaching is a difficult job. Though you may experience occasional "failures," look at them as learning experiences and, once again, focus on your successes!

- Try new strategies. A new teaching model may be just what you need to break out of that rut.

- Understand that you cannot protect your students from society's ills.

- Learn stress-reduction techniques. Take time to pursue a hobby and be with your family and friends. Have fun, exercise, take comfort in your religion.

- Take care of yourself.

- Try not to consider your job as your identity. You are not only a teacher. You are a mother, father, sister, brother, musician, and best friend.

- Change grade levels. Perhaps your personal style is better suited to younger or older students.

- Develop and maintain a great sense of humor.

For More Information

Inner Simplicity: 100 Ways to Regain Peace and Nourish Your Soul. Elaine St. James; Hyperion Publishers; ISBN 0-7868-8097-X.
Learn to Relax: Proven Techniques for Reducing Stress, Tension, and Anxiety for Peak Performance. C. Eugene Walker, Ph.D.; Berkley Books; ISBN 0-425-12776-1.
Silent Power. Stuart Wilde; Hay House, Inc.; ISBN 1-56170-536-5.

Chapter 9
Queen's Safe School Components

Violence in the schools in the United States has dropped steadily during the past decade. Unfortunately, there have been several severe cases, Littleton being the major one, where the violence has been so severe that the nation has been placed in a state of shock. With such a degree of violence occurring in the schools, every school system in the United States has been directed to develop a safe school plan. As a teacher you will be involved in either helping to design the plan, or you will be instrumental in the process of implementation when necessary. Familiarize yourself with some of the basic issues that may be included in the plan by going through Queen's Safe School Components.

1. **Knowledge of School Violence**
     - In general, schools have become less violent over the last decade.
     - The problems in public schools are changing rapidly.
     - Drug and alcohol abuse are a serious problem in both secondary and elementary schools in urban, suburban, and rural areas.
     - Physical conflicts, poverty, weapons possession, vandalism, and verbal abuse of teachers are becoming more severe.
     - The increase in isolated, severe school violence may be attributed to the increase in violence in society among young people.
     - The increase in isolated, severe school violence may be attributed to the increase in violence in the workplace.
     - The increase in school violence may be attributed to the changing patterns of family and community life.
          - Lack of involvement of extended family members
          - Isolation from parents
          - Lack of socialization
          - Divorce, drug abuse, poverty, physical or verbal abuse
          - Communities that promote violence as an acceptable way to solve conflicts
          - Violence seen as normal and acceptable rather than the exception in communities, schools, media, and the entertainment industry
          - Easy access to guns and drugs

2. **Physical Environment Components**
     - Ensure that the school is well lit both inside and outside the building.
     - Install video or closed-circuit systems in strategic locations throughout the building.

- Mix faculty and student parking at the secondary level.
- Trim shrubbery around all windows and doors to limit hiding places for weapons or people.
- Install weapons detection devices.
- Ensure the availability of access to assistance in classrooms.
  - Intercom devices in each classroom with direct access to the office or outside line.
  - Alternative avenues of exit from classrooms
- Limit access to the building by securing doors and other avenues of entrance into or out of the building.
- Make the designated avenues of entrance and exit centrally located and highly visible.

3. Organizational Plans and Procedures

- Each school district develops a Crisis Response Management Plan.
- Each school develops a Safe Schools Plan as based on the precepts of the district plan.
- Each classroom develops a Classroom Violence Action Plan as based on the precepts of the district and school plans.
- Establish set procedures for emergency situations and practice them.
  - Provide written emergency procedures to administration, staff, and students by printing a student handbook or an Emergency Management Manual.
  - Provide copies of the emergency procedures to all parents, community resources, and businesses in and around the school campus.
  - Develop and implement fire drill procedures to be posted in each classroom and around the building.
  - Develop and implement tornado drill procedures to be posted in each classroom and around the building.
  - Develop and implement regular daily dismissal procedures to be posted in each classroom and around the building.
  - Develop and implement emergency dismissal procedures to be posted in each classroom and around the building.
  - Designate code words for the intercom system to alert school personnel of impending dangers.
  - Develop and implement lock down procedures to be posted in each classroom and around the building.
  - Develop and implement a Threat Management Policy to provide protection for students who believe they are in danger.
  - Develop and implement a districtwide weapons hotline

for students and the community to report suspected persons with weapons.
- Provide a blueprint of the building to law enforcement personnel and fire and emergency response agencies in the community.
- Set procedures that establish high visibility for adults in all areas of the school during school and at after-school activities.

4. School Climate
- High academic standards for all students are in place.
- Innovative teaching with differentiated instructional strategies is used.
- Building environment is inviting, clean, and colorful.
- The campus is free of weapons.
- The climate suppresses violent behaviors.
- Violent students are targeted.
- The school environment discredits violence.
- The school encourages students to abstain from violent acts.
- The needs of all students are met.
- Basic nutritional needs for all students are met.
- The climate encourages positive and lasting relationships for students and staff.
- The school carries out partnerships with parents and the community.
- Support services are in place for students who are failing academically.
    - Exceptional children's services
    - Academic support classes
    - Alternative diploma programs
- There are support services for students with behavioral difficulties.
    - Behavior labs - elementary
    - Chill outs - ISS/ICU
    - Control rooms - secondary
    - On-site counseling services
- The school establishes and consistently enforces schoolwide discipline policy.
    - Conflict resolution skills
    - Class meetings strategies
    - Peer mediation

5. Focused Communication
- Notification in writing of all parents of the school's emergency procedures through distribution of an Emergency Management Manual, student handbook, and/or other school publication
- Notification in writing of all community resources and business

in and around the school campus of the emergency management procedures
- Notification in writing of all staff of the emergency management procedures in staff handbooks
- Notification in writing to all students, staff, and parents of the county's student behavioral standards guidelines to include expected student conduct, violations of safe school policies, and the required school actions to be taken
- Required communications between school and parents for
  - Major life losses
  - Major life changes
  - Family history
  - Emotional history (aggression, exaggerated reactions, vindictive actions, isolation, seething anger, etc.)
  - Poor coping skills
  - Access to weapons
  - Obsession with weapons or military
  - Unusual behaviors not previously observed
  - Major change in grades or classroom/home behaviors
  - Major change in peers
- Standard procedures for referral of students to assistance teams at the school level
  - Teacher/staff referrals
  - Administration referrals
  - Parental referrals
- Standard procedures for students/staff to communicate with school administration
  - Communication of threats
  - Suspected weapons possession
  - Suspicious behaviors/occurrences

6. Management of Student Behavior
- Inform all staff, students, and parents of expected student conduct and required school actions.
- Establish a Schoolwide Discipline Plan
  - Outline and specify assistance for students who engage in disruptive and disorderly conduct.
  - Outline and specify assistance for students who are at risk of academic failure.
  - Outline and specify activities that promote safe schools and communities.
  - Outline and specify for students standards of behavior and related consequences.
  - Outline and specify for school personnel standards of behavior and related consequences.

- Outline and specify procedures for identifying disorderly or disruptive students, referring students identified, assessing needs, and serving students identified.
- Outline and specify protocol for safe and orderly schools.
- Outline and specify staff development plan.
- Outline and specify plan for working with law enforcement and court officials.
- Outline and specify how regular communication with parents and the community will be implemented and monitored.
- Require each individual classroom to establish a Violence Action Plan based on the precepts of the Schoolwide Discipline Plan.
- Require each teacher to develop and implement a classroom discipline plan that
    - Includes students in the development process
    - Emphasizes student responsibility for actions
    - Teaches students replacement behaviors for inappropriate behaviors
    - Incorporates student-based solutions and consequences (peer mediation, class meetings, etc.)
    - Deals with minor discipline problems with effective consequences
    - Deals with major discipline problems with a progressive set of redirections, reframing, and consequences that follow the schoolwide policy initiatives
- Never be concerned about "crying wolf."
- Investigate all threats to staff, students, and/or parents.
- Treat weapon possession seriously.
- Implement specific programs with a high level of student involvement in order to curb violence.
    - Conflict resolution
    - Peer mediation
    - Problem-solving strategies
    - Class meetings
    - Community service programs
    - Big Brothers/Big Sisters programs
    - Mentor programs
- Provide on-site support services for students with academic or behavioral problems.
    - Exceptional children's services
    - Academic support classes
    - Alternative diploma programs
    - Behavior labs - elementary
    - Chill outs - ISS/ICU
    - Control rooms - secondary
    - On-site counseling services

- Provide alternative placements for chronically disruptive and violent students.
- Provide intensive ongoing staff development opportunities for all school personnel in behavioral management techniques, signs of violence, trends, and other topics relevant to school safety.

7. Curriculum Alignment/Pacing/Instructional Planning
- Follow guidelines set forth by your state's standard course of study for student achievement at each grade level.
  - Align the curriculum taught in each grade level to match these prescribed guidelines.
    - Specific goals and objectives to be achieved as based on the standard course of study for each grade level/subject area
    - Material selection based on the goals and objectives to be taught
  - Follow countywide pacing guides for each subject area and grade level.
    - "Pacing" is evaluating the goals and objectives to be taught and determining the amount of time that is needed to adequately cover the material presented.
      - Depending on student need, pacing schedules may have to be revised through reteaching or remediation activities.
  - Incorporate into the curriculum topics that cover violence prevention through literature selection, current and historic events, world cultures and conflicts, statistical data, etc.
    - Conflict resolution
      - Class meetings/discussions
      - Peer mediation
      - Problem-solving strategies/ negotiations
      - Restitution
    - Civic values
      - Development of a common vocabulary/ tie to the community
      - Community service projects
    - Community development
      - School interdependence
      - School and parent interdependence
    - Individual class interdependence
    - Cooperative learning
    - Social skills development/competence

- Expressing feelings appropriately
  - Rejection
  - Criticism
  - Peer pressure
  - Anger
  - Feelings of physical violence
- Showing and feeling empathy
- Understanding diversity
  - Cultural
  - Personal
  - Physical
  - Religious

8. Instructional Practices
- Differentiate instructional practices.
  - Clear understanding about what is to be taught
  - Student differences understood and appreciated
    - Assessing student needs through a variety of methods
    - Reading and interpreting student clues about learning needs and preferences
    - Using a variety of ways for students to gather information and ideas
    - Using varied ways students can explore and own ideas
    - Using varied channels through which students can express and expand understanding
  - Inseparable assessment and instruction
  - Adjustments in the content, process, and products determined by student readiness, interests, and learning profiles
  - All students participatory in respectful work
  - Goals for maximum growth and individual success
  - Flexibility as the hallmark of differentiation
  - Use of alternative instructional strategies
    - Project/product oriented assignments
    - Graphic organizers
    - Pictures
    - Technology
- Assess learning styles of students
  - Determine how students learn best.
    - Auditory learners
      - Tend to learn more effectively through listening; hindered by mundane lessons that do not stir the imagination.

- Visual learners
  - Tend to process information by seeing it in print or other visual modes including film, picture, or diagram; hindered by long print passages with little graphic design and long writing assignments.
- Tactile/kinesthetic learners
  - Tend to process information by manipulating objects; hindered by distractions, intrusions to personal space, sitting too long, time constraints, and isolation from peers and other contacts
- Teach to the learning styles of the students rather than according to the preferred learning style of the teacher

9. Time and Stress Management

- Practice and follow routine practices and procedures on a daily basis.
  - Have routines with corresponding procedures for all activities that are performed in the classroom.
    - Classroom entrances and exits
    - Classroom seating
    - Paperwork management for student
    - Turning in assignments
    - What information is required on each assignment submitted and where that information should be located
    - Picking up missed assignments
    - Placement of materials in the classroom
    - Addressing the teacher
    - Addressing peers
    - Asking for assistance
    - Activities for early completion of work
    - Use of materials and equipment
- Employ effective schoolwide/classroom management.
  - Keep students constructively engaged and learning.
  - Set behavioral expectations and corresponding consequences.
    - Use clear and concise language.
    - Provide specific examples of behaviors that will result in disciplinary actions.
    - Distinguish between minor and severe offenses and the corresponding consequences.

- Include consequences for even minor misbehaviors.
- Include sanctions for repeated minor offenses.
- Enforce expectations and consequences consistently.
- Expectations and consequences enforced by
  - Administrators
  - Teachers
  - Teacher assistants
  - Bus drivers
  - Custodians
  - Food service workers
  - Secretaries
  - All other school personnel
- Implement programs to modify student misbehavior.
  - Conflict resolution programs
  - Problem-solving training
  - Social skills training
  - Behavior specialists as consultants
- Establish alternative placements for chronically disruptive and violent students.
  - Continuum of alternatives
  - In-school suspension programs
  - Crisis centers
  - Off-campus alternatives
- Provide intensive staff development.
  - Routine procedures for daily use in the classroom
  - Time management
  - Effective behavioral management strategies
  - Conflict resolution
  - Violence patterns
  - Problem-solving strategies
  - Social skills training
  - Differentiated instruction
  - Engaged learning environments
  - Learning styles

10. Student Assessment/Program Evaluation

- Provide a variety of assessment options.
    - Assess by achievement level
        - Above average, average, below average on each level of functioning
    - Self-assessment
    - Assess by progress
        - Focus on rate of learning rather than level of performance
    - Pass/fail
    - Free grades
        - Substitution for any one grade during the grading period
    - Multiple assessment
        - Achievement, ability, and attitude all measured
    - Extra credit
        - Special projects or assignments allowed to supplement a test score
    - Task mastery assessment
        - Attaining of a certain level of mastery in order to receive a grade
    - Contracts
    - Modified assessment formats
        - Oral tests
        - Take-home tests
        - Extended time
        - Multiple test sessions
        - Project options
    - Portfolio assessment
        - Product/project production collected over a period of time
    - Individualized charted progress
        - Chart, graph, or log progress
    - Advance warning system
        - Weeks prior to the end of a grading period, students given an interim report to show where in the assessment process they are and where their grades stand
    - Evaluate programs.
        - Systemwide reporting
            - Statistical reports of academic strengths and needs
            - Statistical reports of school violence indicators and their percentages of occurrence

- Survey results
  - Community reactions
  - Individual school reactions
  - Individual school personnel reactions
  - Individual student reactions
- Advisory groups/oversight committees
  - Review and evaluate
    - Student achievement
    - Crisis responses
    - Violence prevention strategies
    - Violent incident reports
    - Alternative placements

11. Crisis Prevention, Intervention, and Management

- Essential elements
  - Safe and secure physical environment both in and outside the school
  - Set procedures to address as many crisis scenarios as possible
    - Safe Schools Plan
    - Classroom Violence Action Plan
    - Emergency Management Manual
      - Dismissal
      - Alternative exits from building
      - Fire
      - Tornado
      - Bomb threat
    - Threat management policy
- School climate that reflects high academic achievement, engaged learning, intolerance for violence, and alternative programming for academic and behavioral failure
- Communication procedures clear and open to the community, parents, school staff, and students
- Districtwide and schoolwide behavior management plans that are clear and concise in expressing expected behaviors and corresponding consequences
- Curricula that address the standard course of study and incorporate the concepts of violence prevention as part of the instructional process
- Instruction and assessment that provide for differentiation in student learning and instructional strategies
- Effective management of classroom/school time through the establishment of routine procedures and practices

• Periodic program evaluations with input from the community, schools, school personnel, students, and parents

For More Information

www.responsiblediscipline.com (J. Allen Queen's
    website on responsible discipline and
    safe schools)

Glossary

Advanced organizers a teaching strategy in which abstract concepts from the following lesson are presented at the beginning; these concepts are used later in the lesson to encourage connectivity

Affective domain one of the three main learning domains; deals with the connection of students' attitudes and personalities as they relate to learning

Auditory learning one of the main learning styles; learning through hearing

Authentic assessment encompasses evaluation methods that assess the "real-world" application of skills

Block scheduling refers to alternative methods of scheduling the school year; for instance, creating "blocks" of ninety-minute classes

Bloom's taxonomy Benjamin Bloom's learning hierarchy; indicates that learning begins with basic memorization and builds to application and synthesis of ideas

Bribes material offerings in exchange for specific behavioral or academic performance; can lead to students desiring to do things only if they receive something material in return

Burnout a state of extreme frustration and exhaustion in which teachers feel as if they have no life outside of the school or classroom

Checking station a place set aside in the classroom for students to (self-) check their work

Classroom management everything dealing with the running of a classroom; primarily focuses on discipline (expectations, procedures, consequences)

Cognitive domain one of the three main learning domains; deals with the thought processes of students and their learning

Consequences what happen when students choose not to follow an expectation or rule

Contact log a form for documentation of parent contact; includes name of student, reason for contact, time and date of contact, and results of contact

Cooperative learning a teaching strategy in which students work together to complete a task; ideally, interdependence is fostered

Expectations the behaviors expected of students on a daily basis in the classroom; sometimes referred to as "rules"

Goals broad learning concepts

Graphic organizers ways of organizing information into a type of picture or map format (such as a Venn diagram)

Group investigation a teaching strategy that promotes investigation and data gathering by groups of students

Inquiry a teaching strategy that encourages curiosity of students; involves the investigation of a problem

Instructional strategies methods of teaching that enhance students' learning

Instructional units compilations of integrated learning concepts taught together; for instance, a novel unit that teaches figurative language, irregular verbs, and characterization

Kinesthetic learning style one of the three main learning styles; deals with hands-on learning

Learning styles the various ways in which students learn; the three main learning styles are visual, auditory, and kinesthetic

Mentor an admired professional who is available for advice; can be assigned

Mnemonics learning methods used to assist retaining of concepts; for example, "HOMES" can be used to remember the Great Lakes (Huron, Ontario, Michigan, Erie, and Superior)

Objectives statements of the desired learning outcomes

Pacing guide a chronological plan used to organize the school year, week, day, or class

Positive reinforcement teacher actions that encourage students to do their best and evoke pride in students' own work; praise for a job well-done; it is not revealed to students prior to the learning or behavior being reinforced

Procedures the ways classroom activities are done

Professional relationships relationships with colleagues, administrators, staff, students, and parents

Psychomotor domain one of the three main domains of learning; deals with hands-on learning

Rewards similar to positive reinforcement, yet not as powerful because they tend to encourage extrinsic motivation

Role playing a teaching strategy in which students act out situations in order to understand alternate viewpoints and practice problem-solving skills

Rubrics formats for grading that define exactly how points count

Selective grading choosing the most important items to grade in an activity rather than grading it in its entirety

Simulations a teaching strategy in which a situation is mimicked; for instance, a video simulation of flight

Standardized testing state or federally mandated tests used to evaluate student achievement; typically objective in nature, with a writing section

Synectics a teaching strategy in which analogies are used to foster higher-level thinking skills

Thinking maps a type of advanced organizer that partners a specific organizer with a specific higher-level thinking skill; provides ways for students to connect abstract ideas to concrete visual "maps"

Visual learning style one of the three main learning styles; deals with seeing material to be learned

Index